Saving Humanity

H. Dan Rice

Contents

Introduction

This writing is a plea for the lives of my grandchildren and their grandchildren and for all future generations of humanity. I was born in 1943. My generation has been on this earth for 77 years. The accomplishments and advances made by my generation are many and notable. But as I ponder my lifespan, I realize that my generation failed miserably with its most important responsibilities.

- **My generation failed to make this world a safer place**

- **My generation failed to adequately preserve our habitat, and**

- **My generation failed to overcome racism and bigotry.**

Unfortunately, my children's generation is also failing. In fact, current generations are far more capable, and far more likely, to cause

"Apocalyptic" events than any previous generation. Furthermore, as more and more people populate the earth, "man-made" problems will become increasingly more common and increasingly more difficult to deal with.

If we are to have a lasting peace without war and human suffering, if we are to preserve our planet for posterity, and if we are to eliminate racism and bigotry from our society, then we must examine the root causes of my generation's failures to determine why we failed, and use that knowledge to determine what changes must occur. That analysis is the content of this writing and is hereby offered to the youth of the world and to their progeny as an alternative path toward a better and safer world.

I ask the reader's indulgence should I sometimes state the obvious, should I sometimes offend, and should I sometimes include actions that are already being done by responsible individuals, but what is included herein is necessary to fully understand the problems we face, and guide us to the only plausible way that future generations can successfully overcome my generation's failures.

If we ever expect to achieve a world of peaceful coexistence for all of mankind, we must radically change the entire human intellect. This can only be done by future generations whose minds are prepared to solve these problems and whose minds are not poisoned with misinformation and seeds of hatred.

Prologue

In a hospital somewhere two mothers giving birth
experience complications and die within minutes
of one another. Their babies are taken to the
nursery. The babies have similar features and the
tags on the two babies are accidentally mixed. The
parents unknowingly take home a baby that is not
biologically theirs. Twenty years later those babies
meet as enemies in the desert, each armed with
automatic rifles and grenades. One throws a
grenade and mortally wounds the other, but
before dying the wounded man fatally shoots the
other. Two young men lie dead on the desert, one
Jew and one Muslim. Ironically, the Jew was born
of Muslim parents and the Muslim was born of
Jewish parents.

*It is important that we understand the source of
this hatred and how it passes from generation to
generation.*

Sixty years ago, in America, a young man set fire
to a church. An unexpected explosion occurred,
and the arsonist was seriously wounded and
temporarily blinded. His moans are heard by
another casualty crawling from the church. The
wounded and blinded man is dragged from

danger by the other. They both eventually recover in separate wings of a hospital, and never see each other again.

Several years later two elderly men in a nursing home have lost their sight. As they sit in their wheelchairs by a window, they share stories of their family, their time as soldiers in a far-off war, and important events in their lives. They become friends. One day one of the men tells of dragging a man from a burning church, and the other man realizes that this is the person who saved his life. He expressed his gratitude and thanked him profusely for stopping and dragging him from the burning church. The other says "I am sure you would do the same if you were me", but he also tells the man he did not just "stop by" but was inside the church when the explosion occurred. It was at this moment that the arsonist realized that he owed his life to a black man. He never sat at that window again.

It is imperative that we understand the deep-rooted source of racism and how blindness to color brings races together.

Around the globe, powerful nations race to build bigger bombs, faster missiles, and all sorts of new ways to kill people. Please pause for a moment and think:

Are we on the right path? To what end will this come?

The Planet Earth and the Impact of Mankind

No matter what your belief may be as to the origins of mankind, in the beginning, man was an inconsequential occupant of this planet. A tiny speck on the surface of the earth. But the superior capacity of the human brain to learn and think allowed man to proliferate above all other species.

It took over 200,000 years for the earth's population to reach one billion people circa 1804, but during my current 76-year lifespan (~ one human generation) the earth's population nearly quadrupled from 2.1 billion in 1943 to 7.8 billion in 2019. The population will likely double again through the next generation, and there may be more than 15 billion people on our planet before the end of this century. We must also add to that the ever-increasing life expectancy of the earth's populace and it becomes obvious that the demands for housing, water, food, and natural resources could be 2–3 times greater than the current demand. The rapidly increasing population will present tremendous challenges to peace and prosperity on earth.

This is especially important to know and understand – *"the human intellect and exponential growth in population advanced civilization to the point that the surface of the earth and all life thereon are now largely controlled by, and at the mercy of, mankind"*. Worldwide communications and telecasts are nearly instantaneous, and man can travel halfway around the world in a matter of hours or send a missile that same distance in a matter of minutes. No longer can communities separated by borders or oceans be completely independent of one another. The world is now a global community and is becoming more so each day.

Tribe - A social division in a traditional society consisting of families or communities linked by social, economic, religious, or blood ties, with a common culture and dialect, typically having a recognized leader. Tribalism is the behavior and attitudes that stem from strong loyalty to one's own tribe or social group.

Nationalism – Devotion to the interests or culture of a nation-state. The belief that nations will benefit from acting independently rather than collectively, emphasizing national rather than international goals.

Globalism - The idea that events in one country cannot be separated from those in another and that economic and foreign policy should be planned in an international way.

Throughout man's history on earth, tribalism and nationalism have prevailed. For the very survival of mankind, these concepts must yield to global considerations that accommodate the changes that have been brought about by the ever-growing population of mankind and the rapid advancement in technology, communications, travel, trade, and warfare.

Global Issues and Challenges

<u>Wars</u> - Wars have become an accepted constant. At any time during my lifetime (76 years) there have been war(s) somewhere on the globe, and that situation is not improving. In fact, recent military machinery advancements and escalations among the superpowers suggest we are entering an even more perilous time. Political differences, religious differences, territorial conquests, border disputes, control of natural resources, power, corruption, and greed continue to fuel these conflicts.

A push of a button can send missiles around the globe to obliterate the surface of the earth. There are now in existence over 14,000 nuclear warheads, any one of which could level New York City, Beijing, Moscow, London, or any other major city in the world. Not to be left out, more and more countries are developing and building nuclear weapons to counter the influence or threat of those that already have them. This is only natural and will continue to happen despite the wishes of those that already have them. And now one country is developing a mega bomb that when detonated near a coastline would cause a tidal wave and radiation that could annihilate a huge portion of the entire continental coastline. Although there is a treaty in place that prevents weapons of mass destruction in space (nuclear, biological, etc.), the capability to deliver these weapons from space already exists and one must wonder how long it will be before that treaty is violated or circumvented, if not already. This is what the <u>uncontrollable</u> pursuit of military deterrence brings upon us. With more and more countries with nuclear capabilities, more and more numbers of nuclear weapons, an ever increasing devastation capability of newer weapons, and nefarious groups that would like to obtain these weapons by any means, the risk of a nuclear apocalypse is ever increasing. Humanity seems determined to self-destruct. How do we stop this?

Moment by moment the very existence of mankind is at the mercy of those that control these weapons. Mankind has achieved the means to destroy itself, and all life on earth.

<u>Climate Change</u> - Scientists have long been aware of the cyclical variations of earth's climate, but these cycles typically occur over thousands of years. But scientists now tell us that human

caused contamination of the air from burning fossil fuels and other factors such as deforestation have tipped the scales of nature toward global warming. As warming occurs over the next few decades sea levels will rise and encroach on coastal cities, causing catastrophic physical and financial damage and forcing hundreds of millions of people inland. In other areas fertile cropland may become arid and storms will become more frequent and more violent. Warming oceans may adversely affect whole fisheries that are now vital food sources. If not checked now, these things will happen during my grandchildren's lifetime, and for them and future generations the severity of events will be determined by how quickly and effectively we act now.

Simply put, the downside effects of ignoring global warming are enormous, and to deny documented global warming trends is irresponsible.

<u>Global Terrorism</u> - Terrorism is the use of indiscriminate violence to create terror and fear among masses to achieve a religious or political aim. It may be spawned by a real or perceived injustice that the terrorists believe can only be resolved by indiscriminate killing. Terrorist groups sometime receive funding and weaponry from

nations that see benefit to themselves by supporting terrorist activities. Terrorists can be killed. But to stop global terrorism, we must understand the terrorist's perceived injustice and resolve differences through peaceful means.

<u>Clean Water</u> - According to the World Health Organization, nearly 30% of the world's population does not have safe drinking water, and by 2025 half of the world's population will live in water stressed areas. As the world continues to populate, the demand for water will increase proportionately. Human depletion and contamination of the planet's principle fresh water supplies with pollutants and invasive species does not help. We must become better managers of this most valuable resource and make safe water available to all people.

<u>Poverty & Food</u> - Considerable progress has been made in recent years to reduce world poverty, but there is much to be done. A significant part of the world's population lives in poverty and are faced with hunger even today. A growing population only increases the urgency to solve the world food supply issue.

Children, no matter their nationality, race, or where they live, should not be starving.

<u>Pandemic Diseases</u> – The world has been plagued with pandemic disease for thousands of years, causing enormous loss of life around the globe. On the positive side medical science has advanced significantly and caregivers are better prepared to diagnose and treat these diseases. On the negative side, extensive global travel and increasing populations provide the means for any disease to propagate worldwide easily and quickly, and nations are not adequately prepared to handle a rapidly spreading disease. Early diagnosis and countermeasures are critical.

War, climate change, terrorism, providing food and water for everyone, and pandemic diseases are prime examples of global issues where protectionism and nationalism must be set aside for the long-term survival and betterment of all mankind on our planet.

If I were God, I would be looking down on earth and saying, "What is wrong with those idiots? I give them a paradise and they destroy it!"

Why My Generation Failed -The Negative Forces

Before we can address and solve these global problems, we should identify and recognize the forces that contributed to the failure of my generation.

<u>Nationalism</u> – Nationalism, without compromise, is counterproductive to solving global issues. We should all take pride in our country, our history, our forefathers, etc., but not to the point that it ignores the needs of the planet and its populace on issues as described above. These are problematic issues of our global community, of which we all are a part, and everyone must participate in finding and executing solutions. *That is not being unpatriotic, that is common sense.*

<u>Leaders</u> – Today, it is imperative that leaders of all nations understand both national and global issues. Leaders (and nations) that ignore pressing global issues, as described above, stand in the way of human progress and world peace, especially if they are leaders of major highly developed countries. Nations must carefully select their

leaders to not only lead their nation, but also to act with other world leaders to solve global issues. Local leaders and business leaders must also be cognizant of global issues and be supportive to solving global problems.

<u>Ignorance</u> – Ignorance is the lack of knowledge or information. Those living in the far reaches of undeveloped countries may not have the ability to become educated on global issues. Their ignorance of such matters can be temporarily excused until such time as education and information is available in those areas. However, those who live where education and knowledge are available, but chose not to learn or be informed, are both ignorant and lazy, and they are also the most gullible to misinformation spread by others with special interests. Such people, by choice, forfeit their right to make intelligent decisions, and through ill-informed or misguided decisions, stand in the way of human progress. Understand, however, that one need not have a high level of formal education to be well informed.

Truth is available, but sometimes requires effort to be seen.

<u>Isolationism</u> – People who live in Iowa or Siberia or a central province of China may fail to see the relevance of global issues and may choose to let others worry about such things. They may say "that has nothing to do with my life". But when their young men are called to fight and die in an unnecessary war in a distant land it quickly becomes their problem. When their Iowa or Chinese farmland turns arid and crop yields are reduced to nothing and their wells go dry climate change quickly becomes their problem. When ICBM's are launched and start hitting their targets, extinction is inevitable no matter where you live. When a contagious disease from a far-off place infiltrates their communities and kills their people, it quickly becomes their problem. So, even in isolated areas, people must educate themselves on global issues and carefully chose leaders that will work with others to solve global problems before they become catastrophic disasters.

Isolationism is naivety and no longer a prudent option for any nation.

<u>Lack of Vision</u> - Because we are all very much involved in our day to day lives, little attention is given to what life might be like for the next generation or the one thereafter. For this reason,

decisions are often made for the benefit of the current generation that may be detrimental to future generations. These decisions are typically made by uninformed short-sighted leaders that are supported by short-sighted citizens. To prevent this, we must expand our vision and always test our decisions to make certain they not only benefit the current generation, but also succeeding generations.

<u>Propaganda</u> – I have traveled to several different countries, including Japan, Brazil, Ecuador, Oman, Germany, Mexico, Italy, Cuba, England, and Canada amongst others. I met good people in all the countries I visited. At the family level, in all countries, everyone is just interested in providing for their children and living a normal happy life. *It is when we move from the family level to the political level that things get distorted*. We should never forget that other nations consist of families just like ours, and it is typically not those families that wish others harm. We should not allow politicians or the media to incite hatred or animosity toward those families. As a young American in the 50's, propaganda led me to believe that all Russians were the "enemy", and young Russians were led to believe that

Americans were the "enemy". Yet a Russian family's needs and dreams are no different than an American family's!

One of my sons and I recently visited Cuba. We were warmly greeted by families that lived in very cramped tiny houses in Havana. By our standards they were poor, yet they opened their doors and shared their food with us. As in any country, the children of Havana were a delight. Yet my government, through nearly 50 years of economic sanctions, has imposed poverty on those children because of different political ideologies.

Our leaders, both political and religious, need to support and bring families all over the world together, not alienate them from one another. Policy should always consider and provide for the safety and well-being of all children and families, no matter where they are located. It is the responsibility of the citizens of all countries to only have leaders that agree with, and practice, that policy.

Propaganda is poison to the mind.

<u>Racism & Bigotry</u> – The Declaration of Independence of the United States of America declares that "all men are created equal". I

happen to believe that is true, but it is also true that all men are not treated as equal, and that inequality of treatment is often based on skin color alone. The idea of racial supremacy has plagued mankind since early civilization. It has been handed down from generation to generation and is still with us today.

Saying that all humans are created equal does not mean that they are identical at birth. They may be different in many ways, including size, appearance, skin color, and sex. They may also be born with different sexual preferences. We know that a small part of the populace has participated in homosexual activities since ancient times, so we know that different sexual preferences have been around for generations. Today's homosexual population is conservatively estimated in the 5% - 6% area, and that has probably changed little over time, i.e. it may be "normal" for a small part (on average one out of every twenty births) to be non-heterosexual. There is no reason to believe that number has changed, or will change, over time. It is as inherent to humans as differences in skin color, and it is likely present in most people's family tree somewhere in time.

Greed – Greed, or the accumulation of wealth, is good in the sense that it drives people and companies to work hard and achieve good things, and bad in the sense that it may lead some individuals or companies to make decisions that are self-serving but detrimental to society. Examples include company owners, CEOs and corporate boardrooms that make decisions to maximize profits, increase shareholder value, pay large dividends, and/or get rewarded with big salaries without due consideration to the impact of their decisions on the environment, their community, and their employees. Unfortunately, self-discipline is too often overcome by greed, so meaningful regulations are required to assure a proper balance between business and the protection of the environment, as well as the wellbeing of the community and employee.

Conscience is often left outside the boardroom.

Religion – To a point in modern history religion served the common good by defining moral boundaries to growing civilizations. That contribution is to be appreciated and not underestimated. However, throughout history conflicting religious beliefs have also been (and still are) one of the major causes of war and human suffering. It is ironic that Christians, Muslims, and Jews all believe in the same supreme being but cannot seem to live together in peace. Crusade, inquisition, jihad, holocaust, ethnic cleansing, etc. are all words that reflect the dark side of religion.

It is unrealistic to believe that eventually all people will be Christian, or all people will be Muslim, or all people will be Jewish, or all people will be Hindu, or any other single religion. Christians will not convert 1.9 billion Muslims to Christianity, nor will Muslims convert 2.4 billion Christians to Islam, etc. So, peace will never come until the various religions, and their leaders, stop professing that their religion is the only path to heaven and instead profess and practice true tolerance for differences of belief and a true commitment to a peaceful coexistence.

Let us acknowledge that we are not born Christian, Muslim, or Jew. Children are taught to be a Christian by Christians, taught to be a Muslim

by Muslims, taught to be Hindu by Hindus, taught
to be Jewish by Jews, etc.

Human Control of Our Planet

 We all have our own personal goals, headed by providing for our families and just enjoying life. But beyond what we do with our everyday lives is what is happening to humanity (as a whole) and "our" habitat (the planet). In the latter half of the twentieth century, through population and technological advancements, humans gained control of earth's destiny. For better or worse, we have the very future of our planet and all its inhabitants in our hands. This was an evolutionary happening, and its significance is not yet understood or fully appreciated by most of the world's population, nor do the actions of most of the world's current leaders suggest that they understand this. After thousands of years we have ascended to this point and it is imperative that we awaken to the huge responsibility of being the sole custodian of our planet.

What do we do with this enormous responsibility? Do we succumb to the prophecies of an apocalyptic future that many would have us believe and continue the path to self-destruction, or do we change our course and build a truly peaceful world? Do we continue to pollute the very air and water that are critical to our survival, or do we change course and protect and preserve those resources for future generations? Do we continue to pass racism, bigotry, and hatred to future generations, or do we change course and pass on and practice the truth of human equality? Do we, both individually and as nations, continue to selfishly ignore global issues that endanger our earth and all mankind, or do we change course, join, and solve those issues? *For the sake of future generations, we must change course!*

I am not an inexperienced youth full of wishful thinking. I am a seventy-six-year-old educated man. I have a lifetime of experiences and observations and I reason through logic. I am not a politician or a world leader, but neither am I blind to the travesties of our world and the direction we are headed. My concerns are genuine, and I ask you to join me in saying:

- I do not want my great grandchildren and their children to be under the constant threat of extinction.

- I do not want them to be sent to war to sacrifice their lives or limbs for any reason.

- I want them to be able to breathe clean air and drink clean water, and I want them to be able to raise their families without fear.

- I want them to live here on earth and not be forced to evacuate to some distant "inhabitable" planet because we failed to take care of our own.

- And I want these things for every fellow occupant of this planet and their progeny.

Logical Conclusions

Logical thinking is the process in which one uses reasoning to come to a conclusion. Problems or situations that involve logical thinking call for structure, for relationships between facts, and for chains of reasoning that "make sense."

Logic tells me that increasing the number of nuclear weapons, increasing the destructiveness of nuclear weapons, and increasing the number of countries with nuclear weapons does not increase the safety of the world's population, nor does the increasing number of countries with missile systems that can deliver not only nuclear weapons but also chemical and biological weapons make the world safer.

Logic tells me that the world's population will continue to increase.

Logic tells me that we have reached a point where our ever-increasing population and industrialization is having an adverse effect on our habitat, just as logic told me that filling my lungs with cigarette smoke was not good for my body long before it was proven a scientific fact.

Logic tells me that racism and bigotry cannot be eliminated until we stop passing it on to the next generation.

Logic tells me that the world's populace will never be one single religion.

Logic tells me that most of today's leaders (and nations) are not ready, able, or willing to do what is necessary to permanently resolve global issues.

Logic tells me that, in the interest of preserving humanity, radical changes must occur soon. Otherwise, history will repeat itself!

A Better and Safer World

Throughout history man has, through effort and ingenuity, turned dreams into reality. If we can imagine the world we would like for our unborn grandchildren and their children to live in, we (humanity) can make it real. What would that world be like?

Imagine a world where all international differences are settled by a court of law rather than on a battlefield or, worse yet, with nuclear missiles. A world in which no nation has a military. A world where weapons of mass destruction are no longer needed and totally banned. No more bombs, no more casualties of war, no more young men and women dying or maimed. No more senseless destruction. A world where the trillions of dollars now spent on militaries could be redirected to benefit mankind instead of destroying it.

Imagine a world where the preservation of our habitat has the highest priority, where we protect and maintain the "house" in which we all live.

Imagine a world where no one goes hungry because of location or politics and everyone has access to clean water.

Imagine a world where borders are just a line on a map and international travel is no different than traveling within your own country. You are simply traveling within your world. Imagine a world where commerce flows freely, without hindrance, from location to location anywhere on the globe.

Imagine a world where racism and bigotry are non-existent. Where the intermingling of different nationalities and races is common. A world where different people and different ideologies meld to create a stronger better world.

Would this be a perfect world? No, it will never be perfect. There will always be local and national issues that must be settled by local courts and a need for local law enforcement. These will be internal "national" issues. But world peace and a healthy planet can only become reality if all people, from all nations, come together as a united humanity with the common purpose of achieving those goals.

The United Nations – A Hope Revisited

By now some readers will recognize that achieving world peace is not novel thinking. It is not an impossible dream of a utopian world that cannot be achieved. World leaders first seriously addressed the need to stop international wars at the end of World War I and formed the League of Nations and the Permanent Court of International Justice. Then, following WW II, those organizations were replaced by the United Nations and the International Court of Justice.

Of 195 nations in the world, 193 are members of the United Nations. Only the Vatican and the State of Palestine are not members.

The United Nations has a charter that clearly defines its objectives and procedures, but perhaps a good understanding of its function and purpose can best be highlighted by the original preamble that still precedes the UN charter. That preamble is shown below.

WE THE PEOPLES OF THE UNITED NATIONS DETERMINED

- to save succeeding generations from the
  scourge of war, which twice in our
  lifetime has brought untold sorrow to
  mankind, and
- to reaffirm faith in fundamental human
  rights, in the dignity and worth of the
  human person, in the equal rights of men
  and women and of nations large and
  small, and
- to establish conditions under which
  justice and respect for the obligations
  arising from treaties and other sources of
  international law can be maintained, and
- to promote social progress and better
  standards of life in larger freedom

AND FOR THESE ENDS

- to practice tolerance and live together in
  peace with one another as good
  neighbors, and
- to unite our strength to maintain
  international peace and security, and
- to ensure, by the acceptance of principles
  and the institution of methods, that
  armed force shall not be used, save in the
  common interest, and

-    to employ international machinery for the promotion of the economic and social advancement of all peoples

Thus, the United Nations was put in place to address many of the global issues we have discussed, and since its formation in 1945 the United Nations has, to its credit, many accomplishments and successes in all areas of its mandate. However, despite the intent of its founders, it has failed to act, or failed to act quickly enough, in its most important roll of preventing wars and human suffering.

Twice now, following the immeasurable sufferings of World Wars I & II, world leaders came together to form a coalition to prevent future wars. In both instances member nations failed to follow through with that most important goal. This failure lies squarely on the shoulders of the United Nations Security Council members and their lack of support and commitment to the UN charter which they, themselves, created. In numerous instances Security Council members let their own national self-interest take precedence over global peace initiatives, opposing the very purpose of the UN Security Council. In numerous instances peace initiatives were too late or not executed because

Security Council members did not lend the support needed. As a result, despite the existence of the institution so wisely created by our forefathers 75 years ago, millions of people have been killed or displaced due to inaction by the UN. Most recently, the United States invaded Iraq on the false assertion that Iraq possessed weapons of mass destruction. Had this been properly adjudicated through the UN, nearly one million Iraqi's lives might have been spared and the region might be more stable today. In Syria, the UN passed several resolutions to help bring peace to that area only to be vetoed by Russia, a Security Council member. The result is over 6 million refugees leaving Syria and a similar number displaced within Syria. There are numerous other examples, including the Cambodian genocide where 2 million people were killed, the Somali and Rwandan civil wars where 1.3 million people were killed, the Darfur conflict in Sudan where 200,000 were killed and 2.5 million people were displaced, etc. And, of course, there is the Palestinian – Israeli conflict, which has been without resolution since 1948, and which serves as a constant source of agitation in the middle east. The United States has used its veto power several times to counter UN Security

Council resolutions that have condemned Israel's use of force against Palestinian civilians.

It seems clear that the UN is not achieving its most important task for several reasons. First, the veto power of the original Security Council members overrides the democratic process of majority rules. Second, the International Court of Justice determinations have no clout. Third, the enforcement arm of the UN is far underpowered to carry out its mission.

The UN can still be transformed into the organization it was originally intended to be. It can provide the avenue to international peace. It can provide the framework and leadership to keep our planet healthy. It can help bring food, water, and sanitary conditions to all. But for these things to happen, we must have national leaders (and nations) that are fully supportive to the role of the UN to achieve these global goals.

While the UN may provide the mechanism for achieving a lasting peace, preserving our planet, etc., it cannot solve racial and bigotry issues. These must be addressed from within the individual. For future generations, the dream of a peaceful healthy world without racism and bigotry not only can become reality but must become reality. Unfortunately, current generations are too ingrained with pre-existing biases, prejudices, misdirected beliefs, and narrow-minded leaders to make this happen, so the challenge is left to future generations.

It is to the youth of today, and to their unborn children, that this writing is directed. They will begin the change. **They are the origins of change**.

The Origins of Change

I am about to be born as a human being. I am but a glimmer in my parents' eyes. I do not have a name. I do not know if I will be a male or female. I do not know in what country I will be born. I do not know what color my skin will be. Nor can I make requests for skin color, where I am born, or what my sex, or my sexual preference, might be.

Through absolutely no effort on my part, I am born. Now I am a person. But I am still not in control. I am still completely helpless and totally dependent on my parents for my sustenance. But something changes. My brain begins to absorb all that is happening around me. For the rest of my life my persona will be molded by what I see and hear.

From the moment of birth, I am learning. I have no knowledge or opinions of my own, so my parents have the power to mold and direct me to be the person "they" want me to be. Parents are my primary teachers and my role models. I will learn from them and often I will mimic them.

I learn new things as I enter schooling outside of the home. For the next several years I will continue to learn and grow into a young adult. Then I may enter a university to further advance my education. Not everything that I learn, or that I am exposed to, will be consistent with what my parents taught me, so there will be times that I must make decisions.

Thus, the decisions that I make for the rest of my life will be based on the combined knowledge of what I learned from my parents, what I learned in school, what I learned through continued self-education, and what I learned from my life experiences.

It follows that in this complex world, humans with a higher moral standard and a higher level of education will, on average, by their actions and decisions, contribute more to the well-being of society than humans with poor moral behavior and less education.

Parents and educators are the primary fillers of young minds and thus they, <u>far more than politicians or world leaders</u>, can change the destiny of the world and what it will be like for future generations. Therefore, it is imperative that parents and educators fill those young minds with content that is consistent with the betterment and very survival of mankind on this planet.

The Foundation of the Human Intellect *- Humans are born with a blank mind. It is what fills that mind that determines the worth of the individual to mankind and to this planet.*

Teaching for a Better World

In the beginning of this writing I stated that my generation failed to make this world a safer place, failed to preserve and protect our habitat, and failed to overcome racism and bigotry, and I described the negative forces that contributed to my generation's failure. Now we will look at how parents and their children can turn those negatives into positives so that future generations will not fail in these most important tasks. Since these negative forces are so deeply rooted in our current society, changes can only begin with the youth of today and be carried forward by their children and succeeding generations. So, let us begin with what the youth of today and future parents must teach their children.

<u>Nationalism and Globalism</u> – Continue to teach your children national pride and to respect and honor all of those historical figures and heroes that made your country great, but also teach them about how the world is rapidly changing, and how we are, with each new day, becoming more and more a global community. Teach them about the impact of the ever-increasing population and advancing technologies that are

bringing about this change. Teach them to learn and know about global issues and to know when pure nationalism must be replaced by global cooperation for the betterment of all mankind.

<u>Leaders</u> – Teach your children the importance of selecting leaders who understand both national and global issues, and leaders who will actively participate in solving not only national issues, but also global problems. The importance of good leadership cannot be overemphasized, and it must occur from the ground up, i.e. community leaders to national leaders, labor leaders to CEOs, etc. Make certain the leaders you support have a vision that includes the well-being of future generations. Not only can uninformed or misguided leaders inhibit world progress, they can cause great damage to humanity and our habitat.

<u>Ignorance</u> – Teach your children the importance of education. Explain to them that education is the foundation on which they will make important decisions throughout their life, including the selection of leaders. Tell them that being educated will make them better prepared for parenthood. Tell them that even those who are unable to pursue, or chose not to pursue, higher levels of education must keep themselves

informed and educated of national and global events and issues. Tell them that ignorance due to laziness is inexcusable. Explain the need for them to be a contributing citizen of the world, and not a burden.

<u>Isolationism</u> – Explain to your children the dangers of isolationist thinking. Explain to them why they must, no matter where they live, stay abreast of international developments, so they can, through their own involvement and vote, ensure the ongoing efforts to maintain world peace, protect our habitat, and promote international cooperation. Tell them that if they, and others like them, chose to leave such matters to others, then bad things can happen that may directly affect them, including their way of life or even their death.

<u>Propaganda</u> – Tell your children about the dangers of propaganda. Explain to them that propaganda is everywhere and how television, the internet and social media have provided the means to instantaneously spread propaganda. Tell them that they should be reluctant to take controversial claims and statements at face value, regardless of the source. Tell them not to accept statements as fact just because it is what pleases them. Tell

them to seek truth through challenge and research and tell them how important decisions in their life must be based on fact and truth, and not on someone else's propaganda.

Racism and Bigotry – If you are a young adult, then you have an opportunity to assure racism is not passed on to your progeny. To do so you must teach your children that not only are all men created equal, but also, they should be treated as equals. Teach them that newborns of all races start equal, but some, especially the poor, are not given equal education and equal opportunity. Those children who are subject to those circumstances, regardless of race, sometimes will not be as good of a citizen as those who do have equal education and equal opportunity. The task is to provide equal education and equal opportunity to all. Then many of those problems we often associate with "racial" will diminish or even disappear.

If you are a young adult and you have, for whatever reason or from whatever source, tendencies toward racism or bigotry, then I ask you first to consider and rethink the basis for those tendencies, and second I ask that you not pass those tendencies to your children. As a white

male, I have personal experience with this. I
adored my grandfather (born in 1884) for a
multitude of reasons, but he would sometimes
use slang when referring to black people. I never
knew the reason, nor did I ask. I believe that my
parents, born in the 1920's, each also had that
tendency to a lesser degree, but they must have
known this was wrong because they emphasized
to me the equality of people, regardless of race.

Perhaps it is time to stop referring to people by
race or ethnic background. To do so can
promulgate divisiveness, which we do not need.
My ancestry is Welsh and Irish, but I do not call
myself Welsh American or Irish American, I am
simply an American citizen. Likewise, perhaps it is
time for past sins to be forgotten and move on.
Most importantly, we are all citizens of the same
shrinking world and we must look forward to the
challenges of the future rather than dwell on the
mistakes of the past. As your children mature, you
must also explain to them that it is normal for a
minority of newborns to be born with different
sexual tendencies. You must explain to them that
this does not in any way implicate inferiority and
that they should treat those individuals with the
same respect and dignity as any other human. You

should also point out that those with different sexual preferences can be high achievers and successful citizens that often make great contributions to society.

<u>Greed</u> – Teach your children to strive to succeed in all ways, including financially. But also teach them to avoid taking any action to maximize financial gain that might also do harm to the community, workers (fellow humans), or the environment.

<u>Religion</u> – What I will now write is not intended to interfere with your religion, but rather to ask that your religion not interfere with world peace or promote bigotry.

I shall go back to an earlier statement, i.e. children, with blank minds and no understanding of religion, are taught to be a Christian by Christians, taught to be a Muslim by Muslims, taught to be Jewish by Jews, etc. This teaching first takes place in the home, and then in the churches, mosques, and synagogues. Children are not typically exposed to various religious views, but rather are indoctrinated at an incredibly early age to the religion of their parents. Unknowingly, they become biased. I would suggest that the choice of religion, and the choice of which religion, are choices that should be made by a mind that has been educated to understand all choices rather than have a single belief forced upon that mind. At the very least parents should educate themselves about religions other than their own (if any) so that they can intelligently converse with their children about differing religious views. This would be good for the parent as well as the child. At some point in a young person's life he should be exposed to the various religions' doctrines in an unbiased and unemotional manner. Any religion worthy of following should have no fear of this!

At the core of Christianity, Islam and Judaism is a common belief in the same God of Abraham and a common message of morality and brotherhood. Too little attention is given to this underlying commonality and too much attention is given to interpretational differences that have evolved and festered, through generations, into flammable arguments and even wars and death. This is true not only for the different religions, but also within each religion, e.g. Christian Catholics vs. Christian Protestants, Shia Muslims vs Sunni Muslims, etc. Typically, at the center of these conflicts are religious clerics (priests, ministers, imams, rabbis, etc.) who preach radical divisive views rather than tolerance and universal brotherhood, and uninformed minds are their most vulnerable prey!

It is important to realize that divisiveness can be more subtle than many would realize, e.g. when a cleric says that their way (their religion) is the only true religion and the only path to heaven, they are also saying that all other religions are inferior, and followers of those religions have no path to heaven. That is an unnecessary self-serving claim with no proven basis, and that claim is antagonistic to a peaceful coexistence. In the interest of peace on earth, clerics should encourage intermingling with all people, and not just those who share their beliefs.

Any interpretation of the Bible, Quran or Tanakh that creates divisiveness should neither be taught nor accepted. In the past (and even today) holy book passages have been selectively interpreted by misguided clerics and others to support slavery, racism, supremacy, gender discrimination, bigotry and even war. Any historical writing, including the holy books, is a record, written by humans, of past events. The fact that slavery, racism, gender discrimination and bigotry existed in the past and was so recorded in any book, including holy books, does not make those things right for today. As humans we must learn from past mistakes and not eternally bring them into our lives. Your children should be made aware of these mistakes and taught not to accept them in today's world.

During my lifetime I have seen humanity build bridges, skyscrapers, airplanes, and all kinds of wonderful things. I have seen humanity rebuild after horrendous disasters such as hurricanes, tornadoes, cyclones, tsunamis, etc. I have seen humanity travel from this earth and walk on the moon. I have seen humanity unite to stop evil, such as the holocaust and killings of WW II. I have seen doctors and nurses save lives with new advancements in medicine and place their own lives in great danger by treating patients during infectious disease pandemics. By now it should be clear that the source of power for solving earthly problems lies solely within the human mind and spirit.

A Word About Parenting

Parents are first in line to fill young minds. Parents lay the moral foundation and provide the initial input to the thirsty young minds of tomorrow's citizenry. Parenting is the most important job any two individuals will have on this planet, and it is crucial that they are prepared for this task. Some are, and, unfortunately, some are not.

The fact is that the only requirement for parenthood is for two people of opposite sex to have intercourse, the same requirement as any animal in the jungle. But we do not live in a jungle. We live in an extraordinarily complex civilized world and bringing children into this world should require more than just animal instincts. Still, impetuous instincts sometimes prevail, and the results are not always good. All too often children are neglected and even abandoned by one or more parents not willing to take on the responsibility of parenthood. All too often children are living in slums, some starving, others feeding on garbage. All too often children live in homes where violence, crime, and drugs are common. All too often children are exposed to, and learn from, racially biased and/or bigoted parents and grandparents. All too often children are left behind due to a lack of education. And finally, all too often these neglected, abandoned, ill taught children become their parents all over again, and pass those same traits on to their children. Through no fault of their own, many of those children become a problem, our problem.

There are numerous instances where children emerge from these circumstances and become outstanding citizens, but the odds are against them, and their path to succeed should not be so difficult.

Ideal parents should be mentally prepared and financially capable of undertaking the responsibility of parenthood. This is a message that must be transmitted from the parents to their children, and, since we know from experience that message is not always given in the home, the responsibilities of parenthood must also be taught and reinforced in our schools.

In my country there are more and more families in which both parents work. This trend grew from 20% of families in 1960 to 64% in 2019. This is often deemed necessary with low income families. Other two worker families want to provide more for their family, build savings for a better home or their children's advanced education, or save more for their own retirement, etc. Consequently, when both parents work, the child is sometimes left without the full measure of parental teaching and guidance that is critical to the proper development of the child's mind. Therefore, during a child's most receptive and formative pre-school years, it is best if one parent remains home to assure the child receives parental guidance and teaching.

When a child reaches an appropriate age of understanding, parents should introduce their children to civic and government matters. They should emphasize the importance of their participation in the voting process and explain why that is so important.

The single most important job in any human's entire life is to teach their children the things that will make them responsible citizens in a rapidly evolving and ever more complex world.

Teachers Outside the Home

Once a child enters schooling outside the home, parents must ensure that the teacher's (educational and clerical) agenda is consistent with a sustainable, peaceful world for all of humanity. This is not to suggest books be banned or the agenda curtailed, only that the child is educated and exposed to different ideas but not influenced by a teacher's personal bias in ways that create divisiveness among people.

The importance of supporting the educational process outside the home cannot be overemphasized. On a global scale, a proper education of young minds is the single most important task for any nation.

Attaining The Results We Seek

We have identified the reasons why my generation failed to make the world a safer place, why we failed to adequately preserve our habitat, and why we failed to overcome racism and bigotry. We applied logic to our findings and concluded that success can only occur through a radical change in the human intellect, and therefore can only be achieved by future generations, beginning with the youth of today and their children. We emphasized the importance of filling young minds with content that is consistent with peace and prosperity for all mankind, and we provided guidance on what to avoid.

We acknowledged the efforts of past leaders that formed the League of Nations, and later the United Nations, with the goal of creating a sustained peaceful world and stopping human suffering. We identified why those efforts have fallen short.

We have imagined how we would like our world to be. We know the negative forces working against us and we know we must overcome those forces. It is hoped and assumed that future generations will bring about the desired change as a natural extension of their education (which must include those things discussed herein), and their own logic, but let us be specific as to what must happen.

(1) Future generations will be more cognizant of global issues in our fast-changing world. They will look at the health and wellbeing of all humanity and our habitat from a global perspective. From them will come a new generation of leaders that will enact global cooperation and coordinate efforts to solve global issues, and those leaders will be elected, appointed, and supported by a generation that shares those ideals and goals.

(2) Future generations will create a safe and peaceful world by acknowledging the wisdom of our world leaders when they formed the United Nations. They will use that organization as the basis of achieving world peace, as it was originally intended. They will strengthen that organization by expanding the number of countries on the Security Council. They will eliminate the self-defeating veto and make majority rule. They will strengthen and support the International Court of Justice and insist that all members abide by that court's rulings on international matters. They will

strengthen the enforcement arm overseen by the Security Council to maintain world peace, enforce International Court of Justice rulings, and forcefully deal with any threats to world peace by non-members should the need arise. To discourage separatists, they will institute an "all in or all out" economic policy that encourages trade among United Nations members and excludes trade with non-members.

(3) Once the United Nations begins to function as intended and settles international disputes in a court of law rather than on the battlefield, the threat of international military conflict is removed and the need for massive national military forces and weaponry disappears. The Security Council can then, on behalf of humanity, oversee the demilitarization of all nations, including the banning and destruction of all nuclear weapons and other means of mass destruction. Demilitarization will become a requirement for UN membership and participation in all UN benefits, including trade with its members.

(4) Future generations will elevate the status and funding of the World Health Organization to deal with global health issues, including poverty and global pandemics.

(5) The UN will also oversee, with the full support
of it's constituents, the preservation of our earthly
habitat to assure that future generations will have
clean air, water, and good health.

(6) Each nation will still govern itself in all matters
other than keeping world peace and preserving
the human habitat. Each nation will benefit from
this realignment by enjoying true world peace and
redirecting the trillions of dollars now spent for
national "defense" to things that will benefit
humanity rather than destroy it. Each nation will,
as needed, maintain an internal policing force for
the purpose of enforcing internal laws, but that
force must be sized to do only that, and never be
used against another nation.

(7) A better informed and educated generation
will bring a true shift toward human equality,
stamping out racism and bigotry, and that will be
a strong calming force at both the national and
the international levels.

These changes will not come about easily. Even as
the new generation begins the change, there will
be powerful forces with different views that
oppose demilitarization and thus oppose the
transition to a lasting world peace. With no militia,

the need for military aircraft, naval vessels, missile systems etc. will diminish significantly, and if those that supply and support the military do not refocus their capabilities, they will risk failure and closure. So, the plan to demilitarize should be accompanied by a plan to redeploy those enormous resources to supply and support humanity in more constructive ways. Imagine what positive things could be done with those resources and the redirected trillions of dollars now spent on militarization. The youth of today will also see resistance from certain religious factions, and perhaps even resistance from within themselves. But there are times when one will be at odds with selective wisdom and simply must do what is best for humanity. No matter the source or level of resistance today's youth and tomorrow's generations may encounter, they must not, for any reason, waiver in their struggle for demilitarization and a lasting world peace, nor must they waiver in preserving our habitat and eliminating racism and bigotry!

Throughout history politicians have excited young men's testosterone and macho tendencies and sent them off to wage war. Perhaps in some cases it was necessary, and most certainly in many cases it was not. But we must now move past that and find a better way. A way that assures the safety and security of all mankind. The stakes are now mankind's very survival.

I often see television advertisements asking for support to help those injured or maimed in war. Yes, they made great sacrifices and they are heroes. But, seeing those young men and women that have lost a part of their youth, that have lost their hopes for a normal life, and that have lost their vision or body parts should be sufficient to say **never again!** Seeing mothers mourn their lost sons or daughters killed on some far-off battlefield should be sufficient to say **never again!** Seeing millions of families innocently killed or displaced from their homes should be sufficient to say **never again!** It is time we stopped training our youth to kill or be killed and settle disputes in a better way. That is what the founders of the League of Nations and the United Nations had in mind, and it is time we made it happen.

For Those Who Differ or Doubt

Since this writing is directed to the youth of today and future generations, the biases and arguments of the current generation may be noteworthy but inconsequential. After all, in the areas discussed herein, they (we) have failed. But we must all keep an open mind, and if anyone has a better way to achieve a lasting world peace, a guarantee of a lasting inhabitable earthly environment for future generations, and an end to racism and bigotry, then please step forward and bring your ideas to the public. But understand that those ideas must withstand the test of logic. You simply cannot guarantee world peace by building huge militaries and making more and bigger weapons of mass destruction, you cannot preserve the human habitat by disregarding man's impact on our environment, and you cannot abolish racism and bigotry as long as you pass it on to the next generation.

Epilogue

A Final Plea for Humanity

I am a citizen of the United States, but I write this as a citizen of the world. So, this writing is directed not just to the youth of my country, but to the youth of all countries, the youth of all races, and the youth of all religions. This is a plea for peace and prosperity for your children and their children that only you can make happen.

For the sake of humanity, please discard the thinking of the past and take up this challenge. Then, perhaps you or your children will be the first generation to say:

- My generation made this a safer world by eliminating the threat of war and mass killings

- My generation took care of our earthly habitat and preserved it for future generations

- My generation abolished racism and bigotry

- *My generation did not fail!*